Homemade
Cookies

Homemade
Cookies

Jacqueline Bellefontaine

MQP

Published by MQ Publications Limited
12 The Ivories, 6–8 Northampton Street
London N1 2HY
TEL: 020 7359 2244
FAX: 020 7359 1616
EMAIL: mail@mqpublications.com
www.mqpublications.com

ISBN 1-84072-628-8

Printed in Italy

1 3 5 7 9 0 8 6 4 2

Contents

Introduction

When it comes to the crunch, what could be nicer than the smell and taste of freshly baked cookies? If you haven't already discovered the joy of making your own cookies, prepare to become an expert.

The recipes in this book are simple to follow and ideal for beginners, but there are also plenty for the more experienced cook to choose from. Most cookies can be made using the minimum of equipment, from ingredients that are readily available. In fact, you probably have all you need to make a basic cookie dough already in your pantry, collecting dust!

Cookies are extremely versatile. They can be served traditionally as a midmorning snack or with afternoon tea; popped into a lunchbox or taken on a picnic. Some can be served as a simple dessert, some are great at a kid's party, and some can even be used as decorations—try hanging them from a christmas tree, or using them to brighten up a table setting. A batch of cookies makes a great gift—they look extra special when presented in a pretty basket or box.

The earliest "cookies" were savory biscuits made from unleavened flour and water. From these humble beginnings sprung an infinite variety of treats—thin, crisp wafers or chunky, melt-in-the mouth oatmeal and chocolate chip cookies are popular and available worldwide. Most countries have their own specialties. In this book you will find recipes for cookies of all types and textures, suitable for every occasion, so that you too can bake delicious homemade treats, just like Grandma used to make!

Tips for Successful Cookie Making

Mixing

Once you add the flour, try to avoid overhandling the cookie dough or it will become tough, making it more difficult to work with.

Creamed method: Use an electric mixer or food processor to save time. If using a hand-held mixer, switch to a wooden spoon and finally, if needed, use your hands to mix in the flour to form the dough. The fat should be just soft. If it is too cold, it will be stiff and difficult to mix properly. If soft and runny, it will not whip up properly, and the cookie will be tough.

Rubbed-in method: This can be done in a food processor to save time. If the dough does not come together, turn it out into a bowl and finish binding the mixture with your hands. The warmth of your hands will help to bring the mixture together. Use firm butter.

Rolling and Shaping

Take care not to incorporate too much extra flour when rolling and shaping the cookies. Only lightly flour the surface and your hands.

You may find it easier to roll out cookie dough between two sheets of nonstick baking parchment or plastic wrap, so that the dough does not stick to your rolling pin.

If you find the dough too soft to roll, chill it for as long as necessary in the refrigerator until just firm enough to handle.

Baking

Baking times are a guide only, as oven temperatures vary. The quality of the baking sheet, the thickness of the cookies, and the temperature of the dough when it is put into the oven also affect cooking times. With a little experience, you will soon be able to judge.

Essential Ingredients

A basic cookie is made from a mixture of fat, sugar, and flour. Most other ingredients are added for flavor.

Butter is the preferred fat for most cookies. Even the simplest cookies require butter for an improved flavor and richness. Margarine can be used, but be aware that the texture and flavor will be impaired.

All ingredients must be measured accurately and all cup and spoon measurements should be level. All recipes in this book use medium-size eggs.

Equipment

Baking sheets: Choose ones made from heavy-gauge metal that will not warp or twist in the oven. They will be more expensive, but are usually guaranteed to last longer.

Cake pans: You will only need three cake pans for the following recipes, 8 x 8-in/ 20 x 20-cm square, 9 x 9-in/23 x 23-cm square, and a 9 x 9-in/23 x 23-cm round. If you are buying new pans, consider loose-bottom pans as they will make removal of the cookies much easier and avoid the need to line the pan in most cases.

Cookie cutters: You can cut simple shapes such as squares, oblongs, diamonds, or triangles by hand with a knife. Cookie cutters are inexpensive and increase the number of shapes you can make.

Greasing and Lining Pans

Be sure not to overgrease baking sheets. Use vegetable oil or butter.

Baking sheets: Unless otherwise specified in the cookie recipe, there is no need to line your baking sheets or pans before baking your cookie batch. When required, however, try to use nonstick baking parchment.

Cake pans: Line the bottoms of pans with nonstick baking parchment or line the bottom and sides with foil. When using foil, smooth out the creases. Allow the foil to overlap the edges to make removal easier.

Storage

Most cookies keep well if stored in an airtight container in a cool place. Plain cookies can be kept for up to one week. Softer cookies, filled cookies, and those made with fruit will keep for two to three days.

Do not store cookies with cakes, or crisp cookies with soft ones as they will absorb moisture and lose their crispness. When packing cookies for lunchboxes or picnics, wrap in foil to keep them from picking up flavors or moisture from other foods.

Freezing

Most cookies can be frozen. However, do not freeze frosted or decorated cookies. Cookies that are suitable for freezing should be frozen uncovered, then packed in freezer bags or rigid containers. Many cookie doughs can be frozen before baking. Form the cookies and freeze uncovered, then transfer to freezer containers. Bake without thawing, adding an extra few minutes to the baking time.

CHAPTER ONE

. . . .

Drop Cookies

Traditional Chocolate Chip Cookies

A classic recipe for all the family that produces a chewy, melt-in-the-mouth cookie, just like Grandma used to make.

Makes 10 to 12

1 cup/2 sticks/225 g butter, softened
Generous ¾ cup/165 g sugar
¾ cup/150 g brown sugar, lightly packed
2 eggs
1 tsp vanilla extract
Generous 1¼ cups/255 g all-purpose flour
1 tsp baking soda
1 cup/175 g semi-sweet or milk chocolate chips
Scant ¾ cup/75 g nuts (walnuts, pecans, almonds, or hazelnuts or a mixture), chopped, optional

1. Preheat the oven to 350°F/180°C. Lightly grease two baking sheets.

2. Cream the butter and sugars together until light and fluffy. Beat in the egg and vanilla. Sift the flour with the baking soda and beat into the mixture. Add the chocolate chips and nuts, if using, and stir until well combined.

3. Drop large rounded tablespoons of the dough onto the baking sheets, five or six per sheet, well spaced as the cookies will spread.

4. Bake until golden, 15 to 18 minutes. Let cool on the baking sheets for a few minutes before transferring to a wire rack to cool completely.

Double Choc-Chip Cookies

Enjoy the contrast of white and semisweet chocolate chips in this delicious twist on everyone's favorite cookie.

Makes 14

2 oz/150 g semisweet chocolate
2 oz/150 g white chocolate
1¼ sticks/140 g butter
⅔ cup/150 g sugar
1 egg
½ tsp vanilla extract
1⅓ cups/200 g all-purpose flour
1 tsp baking powder

1. Preheat the oven to 350°F/180°C. Cut the chocolate into small chunks. Lightly grease two baking sheets.

2. Cream the butter and sugar together until pale and fluffy. Beat in the egg and the vanilla. Sift the flour and baking powder together and beat into the mixture. Add the chocolate and stir until well combined.

3. Drop 5 to 6 rounded tablespoons of the dough onto each baking sheet, spacing well apart, as the cookies will almost double in size.

4. Bake until golden, 12 to 15 minutes. Let cool on the baking sheet 2 to 3 minutes, then transfer to a wire rack to cool completely. Store in an airtight container for up to five days.

Orange and Peanut Butter Cookies

The combination of zesty orange and rich peanut butter in this recipe makes for a fresh yet wholesome, tasty cookie.

Makes 24

½ cup/1 stick/125 g butter, softened
Scant ½ cup/100 g sugar
1 egg, lightly beaten
¼ cup/75 g peanut butter
Grated peel of 1 small orange
¼ cup/50 ml orange juice
2 cups/300 g all-purpose flour
1 tsp baking powder

1. Preheat the oven to 350°F/180°C. Lightly grease two baking sheets.

2. Cream the butter and sugar together until light and fluffy. Beat in the egg, peanut butter, orange peel, and juice. Sift the flour and baking powder together and beat into the mixture.

3. Drop rounded tablespoons of the dough, spaced well apart onto the baking sheets. Flatten slightly with the back of a spoon.

4. Bake until golden, 18 to 20 minutes. Let cool on the baking sheets for a few minutes before transferring to a wire rack to cool completely.

White Chocolate and Macadamia Nut Cookies

If you prefer, substitute the macadamias for another variety of nut or pack even more of a chocolate punch by adding some semisweet chocolate chips.

Makes 12 to 15

Generous 1¾ cups/255 g all-purpose
  flour
1 tsp baking soda
¼ cup/30 g cocoa powder
½ tsp salt
1 cup/2 sticks/225 g unsalted butter,
  softened
1½ cups/225 g light brown sugar,
  firmly packed
Scant ½ cup/100 g sugar
2 large eggs
2 tsp vanilla extract
Scant 1⅓ cups/230 g white
  chocolate chips
2 cups/230 g macadamia nuts,
  coarsely chopped

1. Preheat the oven to 375°F/190°C. Lightly grease two baking sheets.

2. In a medium bowl, sift together the flour, baking soda, cocoa powder, and salt. Set aside.

3. Cream the butter and sugars together until light and fluffy. Beat in the eggs and vanilla. Gently stir in the flour mixture until just combined. Fold in the white chocolate and macadamia nuts.

4. Drop large rounded tablespoons of the dough onto the baking sheets, well spaced apart as the cookies will spread. Bake until firm, 15 to 18 minutes. Let cool on the baking sheets for a few minutes before transferring to a wire rack to cool completely.

Coconut Cookies

Rich cookies, with a strong coconut taste. Decorate them by dipping in chocolate or drizzling a little chocolate over the top.

Makes 24

½ cup/1 stick/125 g butter
Generous ¾ cup/165 g sugar
¼ cup/50 ml coconut milk
⅔ cup/75 g flaked coconut
Generous 1½ cups/225 g all-purpose
    flour
2 tsp baking powder

Frosting:
Scant ¼ cup/25 g confectioners' sugar
2 tbsp coconut milk
Generous ½ cup/40 g flaked coconut

1. Preheat the oven to 350°F/180°C. Lightly grease two baking sheets.

2. Cream the butter and sugar together until pale and fluffy. Beat in the coconut milk and flaked coconut.

3. Sift the flour and baking powder and work into the coconut mixture. Drop tablespoons of the dough well apart on the baking sheets. Bake until golden, 10 to 12 minutes. Let cool on the baking sheets 2 to 3 minutes, then transfer to a wire rack to cool completely.

4. To make the frosting, sift the confectioners' sugar into a bowl and stir in the coconut milk until smooth. Spread over the cookies, then sprinkle the coconut over the top. Let dry until the frosting sets, 1 to 2 hours. Store in an airtight container for up to five days.

Giant M&M Bites

These fun, giant cookies are perfect for packing in kids' lunchboxes, as a special treat.

Makes 12

½ cup/1 stick/125 g butter, softened
⅓ cup/75 g sugar
⅜ cup/75 g packed light brown sugar
1 egg
1 tsp vanilla extract
Scant 1⅓ cups/200 g self-rising flour
1 cup/100 g peanut or chocolate
   M&M's or candy-coated chocolates

1. Preheat the oven to 375°F/190°C. Lightly grease two baking sheets.

2. Cream the butter and sugars together until light and fluffy. Beat in the egg and vanilla. Sift the flour and beat into the mixture. Add the M&Ms and stir until well combined.

3. Drop rounded tablespoons of the dough onto the baking sheets, spacing well apart as the cookies will almost double in size.

4. Bake until golden, 8 to 10 minutes. Let cool on the baking sheets for a few minutes before transferring to a wire rack to cool completely. These are best eaten the day they are made.

Banana and Walnut Cookies

You could try using other types of nuts, but walnuts work particularly well with the smooth banana taste of these wholesome cookies.

Makes 20

Generous 1½ cups/225 g
   all-purpose flour
1 tsp baking powder
½ cup/1 stick/125 g butter,
   cut into cubes
⅞ cup/175 g light brown sugar
Scant 1 cup/100 g walnuts,
   coarsely chopped
2 small or 1 large banana, peeled
1 egg
¼ cup/50 ml milk

1. Preheat the oven to 350°F/180°C. Lightly grease two baking sheets.

2. Sift the flour and baking powder into a bowl. Add the butter and rub in with your fingertips until the mixture resembles fine breadcrumbs. Stir in the sugar and walnuts.

3. Mash the banana with a fork and beat in the egg. Stir in the milk. Add to the bowl and mix until well combined.

4. Drop spoonfuls of the dough onto the baking sheets, spacing well apart. Bake until golden, about 15 minutes. Transfer to a wire rack to cool completely. Store in a cool place for up to three days. Suitable for freezing for up to two months.

Spiced Molasses Cookies

Rich and spicy, these cookies are delicious served with a cup of coffee.

Makes 10 to 12

1½ cups/225 g sifted all-purpose flour
2 tsp baking soda
¼ tsp salt
¾ tsp ground ginger
1 tsp ground cinnamon
½ tsp ground cloves
1 tsp pure vanilla extract
1¼ cups/2½ sticks/275 g butter, softened
1 cup/200 g dark brown sugar,
   firmly packed
1 egg
¼ cup/90 g molasses

1. Preheat the oven to 350°F/180°C. Grease two baking sheets.

2. In a large bowl and using an electric mixer, combine the flour, baking soda, salt, ginger, cinnamon, and cloves. Gradually add the vanilla, butter, sugar, egg, and molasses, increasing the speed to medium. Beat for 2 minutes, scraping down the sides of the bowl as necessary.

3. Drop large tablespoonfuls of the dough well apart onto the baking sheets. Bake until the tops are dry, 12 to 15 minutes. Let cool completely on wire racks.

Oatmeal Raisin Cookies

These classic American cookies have stood the test of time. Be sure not to overcook them so that they stay nice and chewy.

Makes 10 to 12

Generous 1 cup/150 g
   all-purpose flour
1½ cups/150 g rolled oats
1 tsp ground ginger
½ tsp baking powder
½ tsp baking soda
¾ cup/150 g light brown sugar,
   lightly packed
⅓ cup/50 g raisins
1 egg, lightly beaten
½ cup/125 ml vegetable oil
4 tbsp milk

1. Preheat the oven to 400°F/200°C. Lightly grease a baking sheet. Mix together the flour, oats, ginger, baking powder, baking soda, sugar, and raisins in a large bowl.

2. In another bowl, mix together the egg, oil, and milk. Make a well in the center of the dry ingredients and pour in the egg mixture. Mix together well to make a soft dough.

3. Place spoonfuls of the dough well apart onto the baking sheet and flatten slightly with the tines of a fork. Bake until golden, about 10 minutes. Transfer the cookies to a wire rack to cool completely.

Ginger Crisps

These crisp ginger cookies look very impressive. You will need to work quickly, but once you get the hang of them, they are quite easy to make.

Makes 20

4 tbsp butter
Scant ½ cup/60 g all-purpose flour
1½ tsp ground ginger
½ tsp ground cinnamon
¼ tsp ground cloves
½ cup/100 g packed brown sugar
2 egg whites

1. Preheat the oven to 375°F/190°C. Lightly grease two baking sheets.

2. Melt the butter gently in a pan, then let it cool but not solidify.

3. Sift the flour and spices together, then sift again to ensure that they are well mixed and lightly aerated. Sift the brown sugar to remove any lumps.

4. Beat the egg whites until they stand in soft peaks. Gradually beat in the sugar. Carefully fold in the flour mixture. Drizzle in the butter and fold until just combined.

5. Place 2 to 3 heaping teaspoons of the dough onto a baking sheet and spread each one to form a 3 in/7.5 cm circle. Bake until just set and beginning to brown around the edges, 5 to 6 minutes. While one batch of cookies is cooking, spread the next one on the second baking sheet. Oil a rolling pin.

6. When baked, let the cookies stand for a few seconds. Then, working quickly before they set, carefully remove from the baking sheet with a slim spatula and place over the oiled rolling pin; they will cool in a curve. Remove from the rolling pin. Repeat until all the dough is baked. Store in an airtight container for two to three days.

Orange Pecan Cookies

When preparing the pecans for this recipe, save a few of the chopped nuts to sprinkle on top of the cookies before baking to give extra crunch.

Makes 24

6 tbsp butter
6 tbsp sugar
6 tbsp packed light brown sugar
1 egg
Grated peel of 1 orange
2 tbsp orange juice
1¼ cups/175 g all-purpose flour
½ tsp baking soda
¾ cup/85 g pecans, coarsely chopped

1. Preheat the oven to 350°F/180°C. Lightly grease two baking sheets.

2. Cream the butter and sugars together until pale and fluffy. Beat in the egg, orange peel, and juice.

3. Sift the flour and baking soda together and beat into the mixture. Stir in the nuts.

4. Drop tablespoons of the dough well apart onto the baking sheets. Bake until golden, 10 to 12 minutes. Let the cookies cool on the baking sheets for 2 to 3 minutes, then transfer to a wire rack to cool completely. Store in an airtight container for up to five days.

Lemon Macadamia Nut Cookies

These cookies have a lovely lemon tang. They are fabulous served with creamy desserts.

Makes 24

½ cup/1 stick/125 g butter, softened
½ cup/100 g sugar
2 egg yolks
Grated peel of ½ lemon
¼ cup/50 ml lemon juice
Generous 1½ cups/225 g
    all-purpose flour
6 tbsp cornstarch
Scant 1 cup/100 g macadamia nuts,
    lightly chopped

1. Preheat the oven to 375°F/190°C. Lightly grease two baking sheets.

2. Cream the butter and sugar together until light and fluffy. Beat in the egg yolks, lemon peel, and juice. Sift the flour and cornstarch and beat into the mixture. Add the nuts and stir until well mixed.

3. Drop heaping tablespoons of the dough onto the baking sheets and flatten slightly with the back of a spoon.

4. Bake until golden, 10 to 12 minutes. Let cool on the baking sheets for a few minutes before transferring to a wire rack to cool completely.

Pineapple Macaroons

Enjoy these soft, fruity macaroons with midmorning coffee or afternoon tea.

Makes 20 to 24

14 oz/400 g canned pineapple
  rings in natural juice
10 to 12 candied cherries
3 egg whites
Scant 1 cup/200 g sugar
Generous 2½ cups/200 g
  flaked coconut

1. Preheat the oven to 325°F/170°C. Line two baking sheets with nonstick baking parchment.

2. Drain the pineapple well and chop finely. Place in a strainer and squeeze out as much juice as possible. Halve the cherries.

3. Beat the egg whites to stiff peaks. Gradually beat in the sugar. Fold in the pineapple and coconut until well combined.

4. Drop spoonfuls of the dough onto the lined baking sheets, piling into a pyramid shape. Allow space for the cookies to spread slightly. Top each with half a cherry.

5. Bake until lightly browned and crisp, 25 to 30 minutes. Let cool on the baking sheets, then carefully remove and store in an airtight container for up to three days. Do not freeze.

Peanut Butter Cookies

You can't get much more traditional than a peanut butter cookie. If you prefer a soft and chewy cookie, bake only until the edges have browned slightly. Use smooth peanut butter if you like a creamier texture.

Makes 24

6 tbsp butter
6 tbsp sugar
½ cup/150 g crunchy peanut butter
1 egg
3 tbsp light corn syrup
1¼ cups/175 g all-purpose flour
1 tsp baking powder

1. Preheat the oven to 350°F/180°C. Lightly grease two baking sheets.

2. Cream the butter and sugar together until pale and fluffy. Add the peanut butter, egg, and corn syrup and beat until well combined.

3. Sift the flour with the baking powder and work into the mixture to form a soft dough. On a lightly floured counter, knead the dough lightly, then shape into a thick log. Cover with plastic wrap and let chill 30 minutes.

4. Cut the dough into slices ¼ inch/5 mm thick and space well apart on the baking sheets. Press a crisscross pattern into the dough with the tines of a fork.

5. Bake until golden, 10 to 12 minutes. Let cool on the baking sheets for 2 to 3 minutes, then transfer to a wire rack to cool completely. Store in an airtight container for up to five days.

Malted Drop Cookies

These have a great malty flavor and a chewy texture. Perfect served with a cup of steaming hot cocoa.

Makes 18

½ cup/1 stick/125 g butter, softened
Scant ½ cup/100 g sugar
1 egg, lightly beaten
1 tsp vanilla extract
5 tbsp chocolate malt powder
Scant ¾ cup/100 g all-purpose flour
½ cup/50 g rolled oats

1. Preheat the oven to 375°F/190°C. Line two baking sheets with nonstick baking parchment.

2. Cream the butter and sugar together until light and fluffy. Beat in the egg and vanilla. Sift the chocolate malt powder and flour together and beat into the creamed mixture along with the oats until all the ingredients are well combined.

3. Drop heaping teaspoons of the dough onto the baking sheets, spacing well apart. Bake in the center of the oven until just golden, 10 to 12 minutes. The lower baking sheet may need slightly longer. Let the cookies cool on the baking sheets for a few minutes, then transfer to a wire rack to cool completely.

Oaty Apple Crunchies

A special favorite with kids and adults, the crunchiness of the rolled oats and moistness of the applesauce gives these cookies a definite moreish appeal.

Makes 18

1¾ cups/175 g rolled oats
Generous ⅓ cup/50 g all-purpose flour
¾ cup/150 g packed light brown sugar
Scant ½ cup/100 g chunky applesauce
½ cup/100 ml corn oil
1 egg

1. Preheat the oven to 350°F/180°C. Lightly grease two baking sheets.

2. Place all the ingredients in a large mixing bowl and beat until well combined.

3. Drop rounded tablespoons of the dough onto the baking sheets. Flatten slightly with the back of a spoon.

4. Bake until golden, 10 to 15 minutes. Let cool on the baking sheets for a few minutes then transfer to a wire rack to cool completely.

Spicy Buttermilk Cookies

The pumpkin pie spice and tangy buttermilk in these cookies lends a sweet and gentle kick. If you prefer not to use buttermilk, yogurt is a very good substitute.

Makes 20

6 tbsp butter, softened
⅔ cup/150 g sugar
⅔ cup/150 ml buttermilk
Generous 1½ cups/225 g all-purpose flour
½ tsp baking soda
2 tsp pumpkin pie spice

1. Preheat the oven to 400°F/200°C. Lightly grease two baking sheets.

2. Cream the butter and sugar together in a bowl until light and fluffy. Beat in the buttermilk. Sift the flour, baking soda, and spice together and beat into the creamed mixture.

3. Drop rounded tablespoons of the dough onto the baking sheets, spacing well apart as the cookies will almost double in size.

4. Bake until golden, 10 to 15 minutes. Let cool on the baking sheets for a few minutes before transferring to a wire rack to cool completely.

Maple Glazed Cookies

These sticky cookies have a soft, chewy texture that children love.

Makes 18

1¼ cups/175 g all-purpose flour
1 tsp baking powder
½ tsp baking soda
6 tbsp butter, cut into cubes
⅓ cup/75 g sugar
Scant ½ cup/50 g pecans, chopped
1 egg, lightly beaten
6 tbsp maple syrup

1. Preheat the oven to 350°F/180°C. Lightly grease two baking sheets.

2. Sift the flour, baking powder, and baking soda into a bowl. Add the butter and rub in with your fingertips until the mixture resembles fine breadcrumbs. Stir in the sugar and pecans.

3. Add the egg and 4 tablespoons of the maple syrup and mix until well combined.

4. Drop small heaping tablespoonfuls of the dough, slightly spaced apart onto the baking sheets. Bake until golden, about 15 minutes. Brush the cookies with the remaining maple syrup while still hot, then transfer to a wire rack to cool completely.

Oatmeal Chocolate Chip Cookies

For an old-fashioned, coarser texture, be sure to use rolled oats. However, if you prefer a smoother cooki , use quick-cooking oats. Add some pecans, macadamias, or walnuts for extra crunch.

Makes 10 to 12

Generous 1 cup/150 g all-purpose flour
1 tsp baking powder
¾ cup/1½ sticks/175 g unsalted butter, softened
½ cup/100 g dark brown sugar, firmly packed
Scant ½ cup/100 g sugar
1 large egg, at room temperature
2 tsp vanilla extract
2½ cups/250 g rolled oats
Scant ½ cup/75 g semisweet chocolate chips

1. Preheat the oven to 375°F/190°C. Lightly grease two baking sheets.

2. In a large bowl, stir together the flour and baking powder.

3. In a large mixing bowl and using a hand-held electric mixer, cream the butter and sugars together until light and fluffy. Add the egg and whisk until combined. Stir in the vanilla. With the mixer on low speed or using a wooden spoon, gradually add the flour mixture until combined. Stir in the oats and the chocolate chips.

4. Drop rounded tablespoonfuls of the dough, well spaced apart onto the baking sheets. Leave space between each one for spreading. Flatten each cookie slightly with the back of the spoon. Bake until golden for 12 to 15 minutes.

5. Remove the cookies from the baking sheets to a wire rack and let cool.

Spiced Pumpkin and Pecan Cookies

Makes 15

½ cup/1 stick/125 g butter, softened
Scant 1 cup/150 g all-purpose flour
¾ cup/150 g light brown sugar,
    lightly packed
⅔ cup/150 g canned pumpkin or
    cooked and mashed pumpkin
1 egg
2 tsp ground cinnamon
½ tsp vanilla extract
½ tsp baking powder
1 tsp baking soda
½ tsp ground nutmeg
Scant ½ cup/75 g wholewheat flour
⅔ cup/75 g pecans, roughly chopped
1 cup/150 g raisins

Frosting:
4 tbsp unsalted butter
1½ cups/150 g confectioners' sugar
1½ tsp vanilla extract
2 tbsp milk

1. Preheat the oven to 375°F/190°C. Lightly grease two baking sheets.

2. Using an electric whisk, beat the butter until fluffy. Add the flour, sugar, pumpkin, egg, cinnamon, vanilla, baking powder, baking soda, and nutmeg. Beat until well combined, scraping down the sides of the bowl occasionally. Add the wholewheat flour, nuts, and raisins and fold in until just combined.

3. Drop the dough in large tablespoonfuls, well spaced apart onto the baking sheets. Bake until golden, 25 to 30 minutes. Remove from the oven and let cool on a wire rack.

4. To make the frosting, melt the butter over a medium heat in a small pan and continue cooking until light golden brown. Remove from the heat and add the confectioners' sugar, vanilla, and milk. Mix until smooth, adding a little more milk or confectioners' sugar as necessary to make the mixture spreadable. Let cool until thick, then spread generously over the cooled cookies.

Tutti-frutti Cookies

*Packed full of fruit, these sweet
cookies are adored by young and
old alike.*

Makes about 24

½ cup/1 stick/125 g butter, softened
Scant ½ cup/100 g sugar
1 egg, lightly beaten
Grated peel and juice of ½ orange
Generous 1½ cups/225 g
   all-purpose flour
Generous ¼ cup/50 g candied peel,
   chopped
Scant ½ cup/50 g candied cherries,
   quartered
¼ cup/25 g candied pineapple, chopped

1. Preheat the oven to 375°F/190°C. Lightly
grease two baking sheets.

2. Cream the butter and sugar together until
light and fluffy. Beat in the egg, orange juice,
and peel. Add the flour and beat into the
mixture. Stir in the fruit.

3. Drop rounded tablespoons of the dough
onto the baking sheets, spacing well apart as
the cookies will almost double in size.

4. Bake until golden, 10 to 12 minutes.
Let cool on the baking sheets for a few
minutes before transferring to a wire rack
to cool completely.

Sour Cream and Raisin Cookies

If your raisins are a bit dried out, plump them up by soaking in hot water for about 10 minutes. Rinse with cool water, squeeze dry, and coat lightly in flour from the recipe before adding to the dough.

Makes 18

½ cup/1 stick/125 g butter
⅔ cup/150 g sugar
6 tbsp sour cream
1¼ cups/175 g all-purpose flour
1 tsp baking soda
Scant ½ cup/75 g raisins

1. Preheat the oven to 350°F/180°C. Lightly grease two baking sheets.

2. Cream the butter and sugar together until pale and fluffy. Beat in the sour cream.

3. Sift the flour and baking soda together, then beat into the mixture. Stir in the raisins.

4. Drop tablespoons of the dough well apart on the baking sheets. Bake until golden, 10 to 12 minutes. Let cool on the baking sheets for 2 to 3 minutes, then transfer to a wire rack to cool completely.

CHAPTER TWO

....

Fancy Cookies

Sweetheart Cookies

These pretty cookies make a delightful gift for a friend or relative. Why not present them in a small basket or giftbox?

Makes 8

1 cup/2 sticks/225 g butter
Generous ½ cup/60 g confectioners' sugar
1 tsp vanilla extract
Scant ¼ cup/30 g cornstarch
Generous 1½ cups/225 g all-purpose flour
5 oz/150 g semisweet chocolate

1. Preheat the oven to 350°F/180°C. Draw four heart shapes on two pieces of nonstick baking parchment. Place ink-side down on two baking sheets.

2. Cream the butter and confectioners' sugar together until pale and fluffy. Beat in the vanilla. Sift together the cornstarch and flour, and beat into the mixture.

3. Place the dough in a large pastry bag fitted with a star tip. Pipe heart shapes onto the baking parchment following the line drawings.

4. Bake until pale gold, 15 to 20 minutes. Let cool on the baking sheets 2 to 3 minutes, then transfer to a wire rack to cool completely.

5. Melt the chocolate in a bowl set over a pan of gently simmering water. Let cool slightly, then dip half of each heart in the chocolate to decorate. Store in an airtight container for up to four days.

Rocky Road Cookies

Makes 20

Generous 1½ cups/225 g all-purpose flour
1 tsp baking powder
½ cup/1 stick/125 g butter
Scant ½ cup/100 g sugar
1 egg
½ tsp vanilla extract

Topping:
1 cup/50 g mini marshmallows
Scant ⅔ cup/75 g chopped walnuts
2 oz/50 g semisweet chocolate

1. Preheat the oven to 350°F/180°C. Lightly grease two baking sheets.

2. Sift the flour and baking powder together into a mixing bowl. In a separate bowl, cream the butter and sugar together until pale and fluffy. Beat in the egg and vanilla. Work in the flour mixture to form a soft dough.

3. Take small amounts of the dough, each about the size of a walnut, and roll into balls. Space well apart on the baking sheets and flatten slightly. Bake until just golden, about 12 minutes. Reduce the oven temperature to 325°F/170°C.

4. For the topping, mix together the marshmallows and nuts. Melt the chocolate in a bowl set over a pan of gently simmering water. Spread a little on top of each cookie and top with the marshmallow and nut mixture.

5. Return the cookies to the oven and bake 1 to 2 minutes until the marshmallow softens. Let cool on the baking sheets 2 to 3 minutes before transferring to a wire rack to cool completely.

6. Drizzle or pipe the remaining chocolate over the cookies.

Chocolate, Hazelnut, and Vanilla Whirls

For these cookies, the dough should be quite soft; you may find it easier to handle if you roll it out on nonstick baking parchment. If it is too soft to roll, let chill for 10 to 15 minutes to firm slightly.

Makes 30

¾ cup/1½ sticks/175 g butter
¾ cup/90 g confectioners' sugar
1 tsp vanilla extract
Scant 1½ cups/230 g all-purpose flour
2 tbsp chocolate hazelnut spread, such as Nutella
1 tbsp unsweetened cocoa powder

1. Preheat the oven to 325°F/170°C. Lightly grease two baking sheets.

2. Cream the butter and confectioners' sugar together until pale and fluffy. Beat in the vanilla.

3. Add the flour into the mixture and blend to form a soft dough. Divide the dough in half and work the chocolate hazelnut spread and cocoa powder into one half.

4. Roll each piece of dough on a lightly floured counter to a 6 x 8-in/15 x 20-cm rectangle. Place one piece of dough on top of the other and press together lightly. Trim the edges and roll up lengthwise like a jelly roll. Cover and chill 30 minutes.

5. Cut the dough into ¼ in/5 mm slices and space well apart on the baking sheets. Bake until golden, 10 to 12 minutes. Let cool 2 to 3 minutes on the baking sheets, then transfer to a wire rack to cool completely.

Melting Moments

These pretty cookies take their name from the fabulous melt-in-the-mouth dough from which they are made.

Makes 20

¾ cup/1½ sticks/175 g butter, softened
Scant ¼ cup/50 g sugar
1 egg yolk
1¼ cups/175 g all-purpose flour
Grated peel of ½ orange or lemon
1 tbsp orange or lemon juice
Mixed candied peel, to decorate
Confectioners' sugar, for dusting

1. Preheat the oven to 375°F/190°C. Lightly grease two baking sheets.

2. Cream the butter and sugar together until light and fluffy. Beat in the egg yolk. Work in the flour and orange or lemon peel and juice to form a smooth, thick paste.

3. Spoon the paste into a pastry bag fitted with a large star tip and pipe rosettes measuring about 2 in/5 cm across onto the baking sheets. Lightly press some mixed candied peel into each cookie.

4. Bake until pale golden, 15 to 20 minutes. Let cool on the baking sheets for a few minutes before transferring to a wire rack to cool completely. Dust each cookie with confectioners' sugar.

Walnut Kisses

When finely grinding walnuts for these cookies, use on and off pulses of the food processor to prevent them from turning to paste. Almonds work just as well as walnuts in this recipe.

Makes 40

Scant ½ cup/50 g walnuts
Scant 1 cup/100 g confectioners' sugar
2 egg whites

1. Preheat the oven to 300°F/150°C. Line two baking sheets with nonstick baking parchment.

2. Grind the walnuts in a food processor until very finely chopped. Sift the confectioners' sugar into a bowl.

3. Put the egg white in a large, greasefree mixing bowl and beat until frothy. Gradually add the confectioners' sugar and beat until combined.

4. Place the bowl over a pan of gently simmering water and beat until the mixture is very thick and stands in stiff peaks. Remove from the pan and beat until cold.

5. Carefully fold in the ground walnuts until just blended, then spoon into a pastry bag fitted with a large plain or star tip. Pipe small rosettes or balls slightly spaced onto the baking sheets.

6. Bake until the cookies can be easily removed from the paper, about 30 minutes. Let cool and store in an airtight container.

Basic Spritz Cookies

Spritz cookies are a firm family favorite and perfect for popping in the mouth at any time. The name derives from the German verb spritzen, meaning "squirt" or to "spray."

Makes 24 to 30

½ cup/1 stick/125 g butter, softened
Scant 1 cup/100 g confectioners' sugar
1 egg
½ tsp vanilla extract
Generous 1⅔ cups/250 g all-purpose flour
Colored sugar crystals, to decorate

1. Preheat the oven to 400°F/200°C. Lightly grease two baking sheets.

2. Cream the butter and sugar together until light and fluffy. Beat in the egg and vanilla. Fold in the flour

3. If using a cookie press, chill the dough for about 30 minutes until firm but not hard. Press the cookies onto baking sheets. If you do not have a cookie press you can pipe the cookies, but do not chill the dough first.

4. Decorate with colored sugar crystals and bake until lightly golden, about 8 to 10 minutes. Let cool on the baking sheets for a few minutes before transferring to a wire rack to cool completely.

Neapolitan Cookies

Children love making these simple but fun multicolored cookies.

Makes 24

¾ cup/1½ sticks/175 g butter, softened
⅔ cup/150 g sugar
1 tsp vanilla extract
Generous 1⅔ cups/250 g all-purpose flour
1 tbsp unsweetened cocoa powder
1 tsp milk
½ tsp strawberry flavoring
Few drops red food coloring, optional

1. Preheat the oven to 375°F/190°C. Lightly grease two baking sheets.

2. Cream the butter and sugar together until pale and fluffy. Beat in the vanilla. Add the flour and mix to form a smooth, soft dough. Divide into three equal portions.

3. Beat the cocoa powder and milk into one portion and mix to a smooth dough. Mix the strawberry flavoring and red food coloring, if using, into another portion. Leave the third portion plain.

4. Shape the chocolate-flavored portion into a sausage, then flatten to form a 2 x 10-in/ 5 x 25-cm rectangle. Repeat with the plain portion and place on top of the chocolate portion. Finally, repeat with the strawberry portion and stack on top.

5. Cut the bar into about 24 slices and lay flat on the baking sheets, allowing room for the cookies to spread. Bake until just firm, 8 to 10 minutes. Let cool on the baking sheets for a few minutes before transferring to a wire rack to cool completely.

Gingerbread Christmas Cookies

To hang the cookies for decorations, make a small hole at the top of each cookie with a skewer before baking. Reopen the hole as soon as the cookies come out of the oven.

Makes 30 to 40

2⅓ cups/350 g all-purpose flour
1 tbsp baking powder
2 tsp ground ginger
½ tsp ground allspice
¼ cup/50 ml molasses
¼ cup/50 ml light corn syrup
6 tbsp butter
3 tbsp packed dark brown sugar
1 egg, beaten

Frosting:
Scant 1¼ cups/155 g confectioners' sugar
1 tbsp lemon juice

1. Lightly grease two baking sheets. Sift the flour, baking powder, and spices together into a bowl.

2. Place the molasses, corn syrup, butter, and brown sugar in a small pan and heat gently, stirring until well combined.

3. Let cool slightly, then beat in the egg. Pour into the dry ingredients and mix to form a firm dough. Let rest for a few minutes, then knead gently until smooth.

4. Preheat the oven to 350°F/180°C. On a lightly floured counter roll out the dough to ¼ in/5 mm thick, and cut out cookies with cookie cutters. Place on the baking sheets and bake until crisp and golden, 10 to 12 minutes. Let cool on the baking sheets for 2 to 3 minutes, then transfer to a wire rack to cool completely.

5. To make the frosting, sift the confectioners' sugar into a bowl, add the lemon juice, and mix until smooth. Spread or pipe over the cookies. Let stand until the frosting has set, 1 to 2 hours. Store in an airtight container up to two weeks.

CHAPTER THREE

....

Filled Cookies

Honey and Lemon Cookies

To make these cookies more attractive, you could use star-shaped cookie cutters, or pipe the filling between the two sandwich cookies to give a more sophisticated finish.

Makes 16

Generous 1⅔ cups/250 g all-purpose flour
1 tsp baking soda
Scant ¼ cup/50 g sugar
Grated peel and juice of 1 lemon
½ cup/1 stick/125 g butter
5 tbsp honey

Filling:
4 tbsp butter, softened
⅔ cup/75 g confectioners' sugar
2 tbsp honey
2 tsp lemon juice

1. Sift the flour and baking soda into a large mixing bowl. Stir in the sugar and lemon peel. Rub in the butter until the mixture resembles fine breadcrumbs.

2. Heat the honey and lemon juice in a small pan until very runny but not too hot. Pour into the flour mixture and mix to form a soft dough. Chill for 30 minutes or until firm enough to handle. Preheat the oven to 375°F/190°C. Lightly grease a baking sheet.

3. Roll the dough into small balls and arrange well spaced on the baking sheet. Flatten slightly with a knife. Bake until golden brown, 10 to 12 minutes.

4. Let cool on the baking sheet for a few minutes before transferring to a wire rack to cool completely.

5. To make the filling, cream the butter and confectioners' sugar together until light and fluffy. Beat in the honey and lemon juice. Sandwich the cookies together in pairs with the filling.

Ginger and Date Sandwich Cookies

Ginger and date makes for a great combination, however, you might like to replace the filling with raisins, or even dried apricots instead of dates.

Makes 14

½ cup/1 stick/125 g butter
Scant ½ cup/100 g sugar
1 tbsp light corn syrup
Generous 1½ cups/225 g
    all-purpose flour
1 tsp ground ginger
½ tsp baking powder

Filling:
Generous ½ cup/100 g pitted dates
¼ cup/50 g sugar
⅓ cup/75 ml water

1. Preheat the oven to 375°F/190°C. Lightly grease two baking sheets.

2. Place the butter, sugar, and syrup in a pan and heat gently, stirring, until the butter melts. Remove from the heat. Sift the flour, ginger, and baking powder together and stir into the butter mixture to form a dough.

3. Roll the dough into small balls and arrange on the baking sheets. Flatten slightly with a knife. Bake until golden, 12 to 15 minutes. Let cool on a wire rack.

4. To make the filling, chop the dates. Place in a pan with the sugar and water. Heat gently, stirring, until the sugar dissolves. Bring to a boil, then reduce the heat and cook gently for about 15 minutes until the mixture reduces to a thick, spreadable paste. Remove from the heat and let cool.

5. Use the date mixture to sandwich the ginger cookies together in pairs. Store in an airtight container for up to four days.

Chocolate Mint Creams

A wonderful combination of clean, crisp mint and warm sweet chocolate. If you prefer you could substitute the peppermint extract for orange extract to make Chocolate Orange Creams.

Makes 18

¾ cup/1½ sticks/175 g butter, softened
¼ cup/50 g sugar
Scant 1⅓ cups/200 g all-purpose flour
2 tbsp unsweetened cocoa powder

Filling:
2 tbsp milk or light cream
Scant 1 cup/100 g confectioners' sugar
½ to 1 tsp peppermint extract

1. Cream the butter and sugar together until light and fluffy. Sift together the flour and cocoa powder and beat in until smooth. Form into a 2 in/5 cm thick log and let chill for 1 hour.

2. Preheat the oven to 375°F/190°C. Lightly grease two baking sheets. Cut the log into slices ¼ in/5 mm thick and arrange well apart on baking sheets. Bake until just firm, about 8 minutes.

3. Let the cookies cool on the baking sheets for a few minutes before transferring to a wire rack to cool completely.

4. To make the filling, place the cream in a mixing bowl and beat in the confectioners' sugar. Add peppermint extract to taste. Sandwich pairs of cookies together with the filling. Store in a cool place for up to three days.

Frosted Coffee Creams

Simple to make with a sophisticated flavor, these frosted cookies are delicious with morning coffee.

Makes 20

½ cup/1 stick/125 g butter, softened
Scant ½ cup/100 g sugar
¼ cup/50 ml strong black coffee
Generous 1⅔ cups/250 g all-purpose flour
3 tbsp cornstarch

Filling:
4 tbsp butter, softened
1⅓ cups/175 g confectioners' sugar
2 tbsp strong black coffee

Frosting:
⅔ cup/75 g confectioners' sugar
1 to 2 tsp strong black coffee

1. Preheat the oven to 350°F/180°C. Lightly grease two baking sheets.

2. Cream the butter and sugar together until light and fluffy. Beat in the remaining ingredients, bringing the mixture together to form a firm dough.

3. Roll out the dough on a lightly floured counter to about ⅛ in/3 mm thick and cut out with cookie cutter shapes of your choice. Arrange on baking sheets.

4. Bake until lightly browned, about 15 minutes. Let cool on the baking sheets for a few minutes before transferring to a wire rack to cool completely.

5. To make the filling, cream the butter until fluffy, then gradually beat in the confectioners' sugar and coffee. Sandwich the cookies together in pairs with the filling.

6. To make the frosting, sift the confectioners' sugar into a bowl and stir in enough coffee to form a smooth frosting. Spread over the tops of the cookies and let set.

Apple and Cranberry Shortcake

These delicious fruity wedges of shortcake are great served as a dessert accompanied by a spoonful of sour cream.

Makes 12

2 tart green apples
1 tbsp water
½ cup/100 g cranberry sauce
¾ cup/1½ sticks/175 g butter, softened
⅓ cup/75 g sugar
1 egg
1 tsp vanilla extract
Generous 1½ cups/225 g self-rising flour
6 tbsp cornstarch

1. Lightly grease a 9 x 9-in/23 x 23-cm round loose-bottom cake pan. To make the filling, peel, core, and slice the apples. Simmer with 1 tablespoon water until the fruit is soft, about 5 minutes. Stir in the cranberry sauce and let cool.

2. Cream the butter and sugar together until light and fluffy. Beat in the egg and vanilla. Sift the flour and cornstarch together and beat in to form a soft dough.

3. Divide the dough in half and roll out one piece to fit the bottom of the prepared pan. Prick all over with a fork. Spread the apple and cranberry mixture over the dough, leaving a small border around the edge. Dampen the edge with a little water. Roll out the remaining dough and lightly press over the top. Chill for 30 minutes in the refrigerator or 10 minutes in the freezer. Preheat the oven to 350°F/180°C.

4. Bake in the center of the oven until golden, 35 to 40 minutes. Let cool in the pan. When cold, carefully remove from the pan and cut into wedges. Store in a cool place for up to three days.

Gypsy Creams

A crisp chocolate oat cookie encases a creamy chocolate filling in these hearty, classic, and wholesome sandwich cookies.

Makes 10

4 tbsp butter, softened
¼ cup/50 g white vegetable shortening
Scant ¼ cup/50 g sugar
Scant ⅔ cup/100 g all-purpose flour
½ cup/50 g rolled oats
1 tbsp unsweetened cocoa powder

Filling:
4 tbsp butter, softened
⅔ cup/75 g confectioners' sugar
2 tbsp unsweetened cocoa powder

1. Preheat the oven to 350°F/180°C. Lightly grease a baking sheet.

2. Cream the butter, shortening, and sugar together until light and fluffy. Beat in the remaining ingredients.

3. Roll the dough into small balls and place on the baking sheet. Flatten with a fork dipped in hot water. Bake until golden, about 20 minutes. Let cool on the baking sheet.

4. To make the filling, cream the butter until fluffy, then gradually beat in the confectioners' sugar and cocoa powder. Sandwich the cookies together in pairs with the filling.

Lemon Thins

The tangy cream cheese of the filling contrasts beautifully with the zesty lemon of this cookie.

Makes 20

1¼ cups/175 g all-purpose flour
3½ tbsp cornstarch
½ cup/1 stick/125 g butter
Scant ½ cup/50 g confectioners' sugar
Grated peel of ½ lemon
1 tbsp lemon juice

Filling:
Scant ½ cup/100 g cream cheese
Scant ½ cup/50 g confectioners' sugar
¼ cup/60 g lemon curd

1. Preheat the oven to 400°F/200°C. Lightly grease two baking sheets. Sift the flour and cornstarch into a mixing bowl. Cut the butter into small pieces and rub into the flour until the mixture resembles fine breadcrumbs.

2. Stir in the confectioners' sugar and lemon peel. Add the lemon juice, then bring the mixture together with your hands to form a soft dough. Chill for 20 minutes.

3. On a lightly floured counter, roll out the dough as thin as possible and cut into circles with a 2 in/5 cm cookie cutter. Arrange on the baking sheets and bake until crisp and golden, about 8 minutes. Let cool on the baking sheets for 2 to 3 minutes, then transfer to a wire rack to cool completely.

4. For the filling, beat together the cream cheese, confectioners' sugar, and lemon curd. Sandwich together pairs of cookies with the filling. Store in an airtight container in a cool place for up to three days.

Strawberry Jam Delights

Children will love helping to stamp out the circles and rings in these attractive cookies.

Makes 12 to 16

½ cup/1 stick/125 g butter, softened
¼ cup/50 g sugar
1 egg
½ tsp vanilla extract
Scant 1⅓ cups/200 g all-purpose flour
6 tbsp cornstarch
½ tsp baking powder

Filling:
Strawberry or raspberry jam

1. Cream the butter and sugar together until light and fluffy. Beat in the egg and vanilla. Sift the flour, cornstarch, and baking powder together and beat in to form a soft dough.

2. Preheat the oven to 350°F/180°C. Lightly grease two baking sheets.

3. Roll out the dough on a lightly floured counter to about ⅛ in/3 mm thick and cut into circles using a 2½ in/6 cm cookie cutter. Cut a 1 in/2.5 cm circle from the center of half the circles. The trimmings can be rerolled and used to make additional cookies. Make sure you have an equal number of circles and rings. Arrange on the baking sheets.

4. Bake until pale and golden, about 15 minutes. Let cool on the baking sheets for a few minutes before transferring to a wire rack to cool completely.

5. When cooled completely, spread the circles with the jam and place a ring on top, pushing lightly together. Store in an airtight container for up to one week.

CHAPTER FOUR

· · · · · · · · · · ·

Bar Cookies

Granola, Date, and Honey Health Bars

Although granola is packed full of goodness, it can be very high in calories. Read the labels of packaged granola when buying to make sure that these bars have all the health benefits of granola without the fat!

Makes 10

Scant ¾ cup/1¼ sticks/150 g butter
6 tbsp packed light brown sugar
¼ cup/75 g honey
Scant 1¼ cups/175 g granola
¾ cup/75 g rolled oats
⅔ cup/100 g dates, chopped

1. Preheat the oven to 375°F/190°C. Grease an 8 x 8-in/20 x 20-cm square cake pan and line the bottom with nonstick baking parchment.

2. Melt the butter with the sugar and honey in a pan, stirring thoroughly until well combined.

3. Remove from the heat and stir in the granola, oats, and dates. Turn into the cake pan and press down lightly. Bake until firm, 20 to 25 minutes.

4. Let cool for a few minutes in the pan, then cut into bars and let cool completely. Store in an airtight container for up to two weeks.

Ginger Oat Squares

A crisp base and a chewy ginger oat topping gives these cookies a fabulous contrast of textures.

Makes 12

1¼ cups/175 g all-purpose flour
1 tsp ground ginger
½ cup/1 stick/125 g butter
¼ cup/50 g packed light brown sugar
1 to 2 tbsp water

Topping:
4 pieces preserved ginger in syrup
3 tbsp preserved ginger syrup
4 tbsp butter
2 tbsp packed light brown sugar
1 cup/100 g rolled oats

1. Preheat the oven to 375°F/190°C. Lightly grease a 9 x 9-in/23 x 23-cm square pan.

2. Place the flour and ground ginger in a mixing bowl and rub in the butter until the mixture resembles fine breadcrumbs. Stir in the sugar. Add enough water to mix to a soft dough. Roll out and use to line the bottom of the pan.

3. To make the topping, chop the ginger. Place in a pan with the syrup, butter, and sugar. Heat gently, stirring until the butter melts and the mixture is well blended.

4. Stir in the oats. Spread the mixture evenly over the dough. Bake until golden brown, about 25 minutes. Let cool in the pan and cut into squares to serve.

Cherry and Chocolate Nut Slices

These moist slices are great served as a dessert. Although macadamia nuts taste wonderful alongside the cherries, hazelnuts would work equally as well.

Makes 9

7 oz /200 g unsweetened chocolate
½ cup/1 stick/125 g butter
½ cup/175 g light corn syrup
12 oz/350 g gingersnap cookies
1 cup/125 g candied cherries
Generous ¾ cup/100 g coarsely
   chopped, toasted macadamias

1. Coarsely chop the chocolate and butter and place in a large bowl with the corn syrup. Melt by microwaving on medium for 2 minutes or by setting the bowl over a pan of simmering water.

2. Place half the gingersnaps in a food processor and process to fine crumbs. Coarsely chop the remaining cookies and add both to the melted chocolate mixture. Halve the cherries and add with the nuts to the chocolate mixture. Combine thoroughly so that the cookies, cherries, and nuts are coated with chocolate.

3. Line an 8 x 8-in/20 x 20-cm loose-bottom square cake pan with nonstick baking parchment. Spoon in the chocolate mixture and let set in the refrigerator for 2 hours. Remove from the pan, peel off the paper, and cut into slices.

Chocolate Caramel Slices

Makes 12

½ cup/1 stick/125 g butter, softened
Scant ¼ cup/50 g sugar
Generous 1 cup/150 g all-purpose flour
3 tbsp cornstarch

Filling:
6 tbsp butter
¼ cup/50 g packed light brown sugar
1 tbsp light corn syrup
14 oz/400 g canned sweetened
   condensed milk

Topping:
4 oz/100 g semisweet or milk chocolate
1 tbsp butter
1 oz/25 g white chocolate

1. Preheat the oven to 350°F/180°C. Grease an 8 x 8-in/20 x 20-cm square cake pan and line the bottom with nonstick baking parchment.

2. Cream the butter and sugar together until light and fluffy. Sift together the flour and cornstarch and mix in to form a smooth dough. Press the mixture into the bottom of the pan. Bake until just golden and firm, about 25 minutes.

3. To make the filling, combine the ingredients in a pan and heat gently, stirring until the sugar dissolves. Bring slowly to a boil and boil the mixture gently for about 5 minutes, stirring constantly with a wooden spoon until thickened. Pour evenly over the cookie base.

4. To make the topping, melt the semisweet or milk chocolate in a bowl set over a pan of hot water. Stir in the butter. Spread over the caramel filling. Melt the white chocolate in the same way. Spoon into a pastry bag and pipe squiggles over the darker chocolate. (Alternatively, drizzle the white chocolate from a spoon.) Swirl with a skewer to create a marbled effect and let set. Serve cut into squares.

Apricot and Almond Slices

For a chewy, jammy, nutty flavor that is out of this world, you can't beat these fruit slices.

Makes 16

2 cups/300 g all-purpose flour
3 tbsp confectioners' sugar
1 tsp baking powder
¾ cup/1½ sticks/175 g butter
2 egg yolks

Topping:
Scant ¼ cup/60 g apricot jam
2 egg whites
½ cup/100 g sugar
Scant ½ cup/50 g ground almonds
Scant ½ cup/50 g sliced almonds

Glaze:
¼ cup/60 g apricot jam

1. Preheat the oven to 375°F/190°C. Lightly grease an 9 x 9-in/23 x 23-cm square cake pan.

2. Sift the flour, confectioners' sugar, and baking powder into a mixing bowl. Cut the butter into cubes and rub in until the mixture resembles fine breadcrumbs. Stir in the egg yolks. Using your fingertips, work the mixture together to form a smooth dough, adding a little cold water if necessary. Roll or press out the dough to fit the bottom of the prepared pan and prick all over with a fork. Bake until just golden, about 10 minutes.

3. Remove from the oven. To make the topping, spread the apricot jam over the crust. Beat the egg whites until frothy but not stiff. Stir in the sugar and ground almonds. Spread over the jam and sprinkle the sliced almonds on top. Return to the oven until golden brown, about 20 minutes. Let cool in the pan.

4. Carefully remove the pastry from the pan. To make the glaze, melt the apricot jam with 1 tablespoon water and brush over the surface to glaze. Cut into triangles to serve.

Chocolate Macadamia Nut Brownies

A classic bar cookie for purists everywhere—true chocoholics might like to serve these brownies with a scoop of vanilla (or even chocolate) ice cream and a drizzle of hot fudge.

Makes 9

1 cup/2 sticks/225 g butter
8 oz/225 g semisweet chocolate,
   coarsely chopped
1 cup/125 g macadamias,
   coarsely chopped
1¼ cups/250 g packed light brown sugar
3 eggs
Generous 1½ cups/225 g all-purpose flour
2 tsp baking powder
½ tsp salt

1. Preheat the oven to 350°F/180°C. Melt the butter and chocolate together in a bowl set over a pan of simmering water until smooth and glossy. Let cool slightly. Toast the macadamias on a baking sheet in the preheated oven until just golden, about 5 minutes.

2. Beat the sugar and eggs together in a large bowl until well blended. Stir in the chocolate mixture. Sift in the flour and baking powder together and fold in. Stir in the toasted nuts.

3. Using nonstick baking parchment, line the bottom of an 8 x 8-in/20 x 20-cm square pan that is at least 2 in/5 cm deep. Pour in the batter and bake until the edges are firm, 30 to 35 minutes. Let cool in the pan. Don't expect the brownies to be set when they come out of the oven—they will harden as they cool.

Hazelnut and Chocolate Bars

Toasting the hazelnuts in this recipe really brings out the nutty flavor.

Makes 12

3 oz/75 g semisweet chocolate
½ cup/1 stick/125 g butter, softened
¼ cup/50 g packed light brown sugar
⅔ cup/100 g all-purpose flour
¾ cup/75 g rolled oats
12 tbsp/175 g chocolate hazelnut
   spread, such as Nutella
⅓ cup/50 g hazelnuts, chopped
   and toasted

1. Preheat the oven to 350°F/180°C. Lightly grease an 8 x 8-in/20 x 20-cm square cake pan and line the bottom with nonstick baking parchment.

2. Melt the chocolate in a microwave or in a bowl set over a pan of simmering water. Cream the butter and sugar together until light and fluffy. Beat in the chocolate, then mix in the flour and oats to form a soft dough.

3. Press the mixture into the bottom of the prepared pan and bake until just golden, about 25 minutes.

4. Let cool in the pan. Remove from the pan and spread with chocolate hazelnut spread. Sprinkle with the hazelnuts and press lightly into the spread. Cut into bars. Store in a cool place, in a single layer in an airtight container, for up to one week.

Cappuccino Bars

Serve up these sumptuous bars at a coffee morning—the sheer variety of textures make for a decadent treat.

Makes 12

⅓ cup/50 g golden raisins
½ cup/125 ml hot strong black coffee
10 oz/300 g graham crackers
½ cup/25 g mini marshmallows
8 oz/225 g semisweet chocolate
4 tbsp butter

Topping:
8 oz/225 g white chocolate
4 tbsp butter
Scant 1 cup/100 g confectioners' sugar
Grated semisweet chocolate

1. Lightly grease an 8 x 8-in/20 x 20-cm square pan and line the bottom with nonstick baking parchment.

2. Soak the raisins in the hot coffee for 5 minutes. Break the graham crackers into small pieces and place in a bowl with the marshmallows. Sprinkle in the coffee and soaked raisins.

3. Melt the chocolate and butter in a microwave or in a bowl set over a pan of hot water. Add to the graham cracker mixture and stir until well coated. Press the mixture into the prepared cake pan and let chill until firm.

4. To make the topping, melt the white chocolate in a microwave or in a bowl set over a pan of hot water. Let cool. Cream the butter until soft, gradually beat in the confectioners' sugar. Beat in the melted white chocolate. Spread the mixture over the graham cracker base and let set.

5. Sprinkle with grated chocolate and cut into bars. Store in an airtight container in a cool place for up to four days.

No-Bake Chocolate Fudge Bars

The beauty of these bars is their simplicity—and their unadulterated chocolate hit!

Makes 12

8 oz/225 g vanilla wafers
½ cup/1 stick/125 g butter
2 tbsp light corn syrup
2 tbsp unsweetened cocoa powder
4 oz/100 g milk chocolate,
    broken into pieces
3 tbsp confectioners' sugar
2 tbsp milk

1. Lightly grease a 8 x 8-in/20 x 20-cm square pan. Place the wafers in a plastic bag and crush to produce fine crumbs with a rolling pin. Alternatively, process the wafers to crumbs in a food processor.

2. Place the butter, corn syrup, and cocoa in a small pan and heat gently until melted and blended, while stirring. Add the crumbs and stir until well combined.

3. Press the mixture into the pan and let chill until firm, at least 1 hour.

4. Melt the chocolate together with the confectioners' sugar and milk in a small bowl over a pan of hot water. Spread over the crumb crust and let set before cutting into bars.

Apple Streusel Bars

Makes 12

1½ cups/225 g self-rising flour
Scant ½ cup/50 g ground almonds
¾ cup/1½ sticks/175 g butter
⅜ cup/75 g packed light brown sugar
2 egg yolks

Topping:
3 Granny Smith or Golden
   Delicious apples
⅓ cup/50 g golden raisins, optional
2 tbsp water
Generous 1¼ cups/175 g
   all-purpose flour
½ tsp ground cloves
6 tbsp butter
⅜ cup/75 g packed light brown sugar

1. Preheat the oven to 350°F/180°C. Lightly grease an 9 x 9-in/23 x 23-cm square baking pan.

2. Place the flour into a mixing bowl and stir in the almonds. Cut the butter into cubes and rub into the mixture until it resembles breadcrumbs. Stir in the sugar. Add the egg yolks and work the mixture together to form a firm dough. Press into the bottom of the pan. Prick all over and chill while preparing the topping.

3. To make the topping, peel, core, and coarsely chop the apples. Place in a pan with the raisins and 2 tablespoons water. Simmer until tender, about 3 to 4 minutes.

4. Sift the flour and cloves into a bowl. Rub in the butter until the mixture resembles coarse breadcrumbs. Stir in the sugar. Spread the apple mixture over the dough and sprinkle the streusel mixture on top. Bake until the topping is golden, about 45 minutes. Cool in the pan.

5. Serve cut into bars or squares. Store in the refrigerator for up to four days.

Marzipan Bars

These almond-flavored bars are simplicity itself to make and are ideal for packing into lunchboxes as they transport so well.

Makes 14

Generous 1½ cups/225 g all-purpose flour
½ tsp baking powder
4 tbsp butter, cut into cubes
¼ cup/50 g packed light brown sugar
4 to 5 tbsp cold milk
8 oz/225 g marzipan
Scant ½ cup/50 g confectioners' sugar

1. Preheat the oven to 400°F/200°C. Lightly grease a 8 x 8-in/20 x 20-cm square loose-bottom cake pan.

2. Sift the flour and baking powder into a bowl. Rub in the butter until the mixture resembles fine breadcrumbs. Stir in the sugar, then add enough cold milk (4 to 5 tablespoons) to mix to a firm dough.

3. On a lightly floured counter, roll out half the dough to fit the pan; place it in the bottom of the pan. Roll out the marzipan to the same size and place on top. Finally, roll out the remaining dough and use it to cover the marzipan.

4. Bake until golden brown, about 20 minutes. Let cool in the pan. Carefully remove the whole square from the pan and cut into 14 bars.

5. Sift the confectioners' sugar into a small bowl and stir in enough water to mix to a smooth frosting. Spoon into a small pastry bag fitted with a plain writing tip and drizzle back and forth over the bars to decorate. Let set.

Tangy Cream Cheese Bars

Cream cheese blends best if allowed to soften at room temperature for a good hour before mixing. Be sure to store these in the refrigerator as cream cheese is perishable.

Makes 18

¾ cup/1½ sticks/175 g butter,
   softened
4 oz/100 g whole cream cheese
¾ cup/175 g sugar
1 egg
2 tbsp orange juice
2 tbsp lemon juice
Scant ½ cup/75 g mixed candied peel
2⅓ cups/350 g all-purpose flour
1 tsp baking powder

Frosting:
Scant 1 cup/100 g confectioners' sugar
1 tbsp orange or lemon juice

1. Preheat the oven to 375°F/190°C. Grease a shallow 9 x 9-in/23 x 23-cm square pan.

2. Beat the butter and cream cheese together, then add the sugar and continue to beat until pale and fluffy. Beat in the egg. Beat in the fruit juices and stir in the mixed candied peel.

3. Sift the flour and baking powder together and add to the mixture to form a soft dough. Roll out on a lightly floured counter to a square that will fit the bottom of the prepared pan.

4. Bake until golden, 25 to 30 minutes. Let cool in the pan.

5. Cut into bars. Sift the confectioners' sugar into a small bowl and stir in enough juice to make a smooth frosting. Drizzle the frosting over bars and let set.

CHAPTER FIVE

. . . .

Rolled and Shaped Cookies

Nutty Jam Slices

Sticky and crunchy, these bite-size slices are enjoyable to make and great for teatime snacking.

Makes 20

4 tbsp butter
Scant ¼ cup/50 g sugar
1 egg, separated
1 tsp almond extract
Scant ⅔ cup/100 g all-purpose flour
Scant ¼ cup/25 g ground almonds
Scant ¼ cup/25 g sliced almonds
Jam of your choice

1. Lightly grease a baking sheet. Cream the butter and sugar together until light and fluffy. Beat in the egg yolk and almond extract. Work in the flour and ground almonds to form a firm dough. Add a little extra flour if the mixture is too soft.

2. Divide the dough in half and roll each into a log about 10 in/25 cm long. Place on the prepared sheet.

3. Lightly whisk the egg white with a fork and brush over each log. Lightly crush the almonds and press onto the logs. Flatten each log slightly. Use the handle of a wooden spoon to press a channel down the center of each log. Fill the hollows with jam. Let chill for 30 minutes.

4. Preheat the oven to 350°F/180°C.

5. Bake the logs until pale golden brown, 10 to 12 minutes. Leave on the baking sheet until the jam has set but the dough is still warm. Cut diagonally into slices and transfer to a wire rack to cool completely.

Domino Cookies

Make chocolate-flavored dominoes by substituting 2 tablespoons unsweetened cocoa powder for the same amount of the flour. Pipe dots and lines with white frosting.

Makes 14

6 tbsp butter, softened
⅓ cup/75 g sugar
1 egg
1 tsp vanilla extract
Scant 1½ cups/200 g all-purpose flour
¼ cup/50 g ground rice
1 oz/25 g semisweet chocolate,
    to decorate

1. Cream the butter and sugar together until light and fluffy. Beat in the egg and vanilla. Sift the flour and ground rice together and beat in to form a soft dough. Let chill for 30 minutes.

2. Preheat the oven to 350°F/180°C. Lightly grease a baking sheet. Roll out the dough on a lightly floured counter to about ⅛ in/5 mm thick and cut out rectangles measuring about 2 x 3 in/5 x 7.5 cm. Arrange slightly spaced on the baking sheet.

3. Bake until pale golden, 10 to 12 minutes. Let cool on the baking sheet for a few minutes before transferring to a wire rack to cool completely.

4. To decorate, melt the chocolate in a microwave or in a bowl set over a pan of hot water. Spoon into a pastry bag fitted with a small writing tip. Pipe domino dots and lines onto the cookies and let set.

5. Store in an airtight container for up to one week.

Coffee and Cinnamon Cookies

The cinnamon flavor and attractive crescent shape of these little cookies makes them perfect for serving at Christmas time.

Makes 40

1 tbsp instant coffee granules
1 tbsp boiling water
1 cup/2 sticks/225 g butter
Scant ¾ cup/165 g sugar
1 tbsp Kahlúa or other coffee-flavored
   liqueur
Scant 3 cups/400 g all-purpose flour
2 tsp ground cinnamon
¼ cup/30 g confectioners' sugar

1. Preheat the oven to 350°F/180°C. Lightly grease two baking sheets. Dissolve the coffee in 1 tablespoon boiling water.

2. Cream the butter and sugar together until pale and fluffy. Beat in the coffee and liqueur. Sift the flour and 1 teaspoon of the cinnamon together, then beat into the dough.

3. Take small amounts of the dough, each about the size of a walnut, and roll into balls. Shape each ball into a log, then curve it into a crescent. Space well apart on the baking sheets. Bake until golden, about 12 minutes. Let cool on the baking sheets 2 to 3 minutes, then transfer to a wire rack to cool completely.

4. Sift the confectioners' sugar and remaining cinnamon together a couple of times to ensure that the sugar and spice are well mixed. Dust the cookies with the spiced sugar. Store in an airtight container for up to five days.

Chocolate Thumbprint Cookies

Kids love helping to bake these chocolate cookies. Using white chocolate to fill the well in each cookie gives a lovely color contrast. Alternatively, try using peanut butter for a smooth, nutty flavor.

Makes 24

2 oz/50 g semisweet chocolate
4 tbsp butter
¼ cup/50 g white vegetable shortening
Scant ¼ cup/50 g sugar
1¼ cups/175 g all-purpose flour

Filling:
3 oz/75 g semisweet, milk or
   white chocolate

1. Melt the chocolate in a microwave or in a bowl set over a pan of hot water. Let cool.

2. Cream the butter, shortening, and sugar together until light and fluffy. Beat in the melted chocolate, then the flour and mix to form a smooth dough. Let chill for 30 minutes.

3. Preheat the oven to 350°F/180°C. Lightly grease a baking sheet. Shape the dough into 1 in/2.5 cm balls and arrange well spaced on the baking sheet. Press your thumb into the center of each ball to form a well.

4. Bake for 10 minutes. Let cool for a few minutes on the baking sheet, then transfer to a wire rack to cool completely.

5. For the filling, melt the chocolate in a microwave or in a bowl set over a pan of hot water. Spoon or pipe into the center of the cookies and let set.

Pistachio Biscotti

Makes 50

Generous 1⅓ cups/175 g pistachios
Generous 3 cups/460 g all-purpose flour
Generous ⅔ cup/125 g coarse cornmeal
2 tsp baking powder
½ cup/1 stick/125 g butter
Scant ½ cup/100 g sugar
3 eggs
1 tsp grated lemon peel
1 tsp grated orange peel
2 tbsp orange juice
½ tsp almond extract
1 tsp fennel seeds, crushed, optional

1. Preheat the oven to 350°F/180°C. Lightly grease two baking sheets. Coarsely chop half the pistachios. Sift the flour, cornmeal, and baking powder together.

2. Cream the butter and sugar together until pale and fluffy. Beat in the eggs one at a time. Beat in the lemon and orange peel, juice, almond extract, and fennel seeds. Do not worry if the mixture looks curdled at this stage, as this is normal.

3. Beat in the chopped and whole pistachios. Finally, work in the flour mixture, using your hands to mix it to a soft dough. Divide the dough into four pieces and roll each piece into a log shape about 12 in/30 cm long on a lightly floured counter. Place on the baking sheets and flatten slightly.

4. Bake until the logs are risen and golden, about 30 minutes; reverse the baking sheets halfway through the baking time. Remove from the oven and let cool slightly.

5. Reduce the oven temperature to 325°F/170°C. When the logs are cool enough to handle, cut each one diagonally into ½ in/1 cm slices. Arrange cut-side down on the baking sheets and return to the oven until crisp and golden, about 10 minutes. Store in an airtight container up to two weeks.

Oat Crunch Cookies

While the cookies are hot, press an indentation into the center of each one with your thumb and fill with a little jam.

Makes 20

Scant 1 cup/150 g all-purpose flour
1 tsp baking soda
1¾ cups/175 g rolled oats
½ cup/1 stick/125 g butter
½ cup/100 g packed light brown sugar
1 tbsp light corn syrup
1 tbsp water

1. Preheat the oven to 350°F/180°C. Lightly grease two baking sheets. Sift the flour and baking soda into a mixing bowl. Stir in the oats.

2. Place the butter, sugar, corn syrup, and 1 tablespoon water in a pan and heat gently, stirring until combined. Add to the dry ingredients and stir until well mixed.

3. Take small amounts of the dough, each about the size of a walnut, and roll into balls. Space them well apart on the baking sheets and flatten slightly.

4. Bake until golden, 16 to 18 minutes. Let cool on the baking sheets for 2 to 3 minutes, then transfer to a wire rack to cool completely. Store in an airtight container for up to five days.

Iced Sprinkle Cookies

Fun and colorful, you could also decorate these cookies with melted chocolate instead of the frosting. Use chocolate sprinkles, too.

Makes 18 to 24

½ cup/1 stick/125 g butter, softened
Scant ½ cup/50 g confectioners' sugar
1 tsp vanilla extract
1¼ cups/175 g all-purpose flour
2 tbsp ground rice

Frosting:
Scant 1 cup/100 g confectioners' sugar
1 tbsp water or lemon juice
Colored sugar sprinkles

1. Preheat the oven to 400°F/200°C.

2. Cream the butter and the confectioners' sugar together until pale and fluffy. Beat in the vanilla. Add the flour and ground rice and mix to form a soft dough.

3. Place the dough between two sheets of plastic wrap and roll out to about ⅛ in/3 mm thick. Cut out cookies using a 2 to 3 in/5 to 7 cm cookie cutter and carefully transfer to the baking sheets.

4. Bake until crisp and golden, about 8 minutes. Let cool on the baking sheets for a few minutes before transferring to a wire rack to cool completely.

5. Sift the confectioners' sugar into a bowl and add enough water or lemon juice to mix to a smooth frosting. Spread the frosting over the cookies with a metal spatula and decorate with sugar sprinkles. Let frosting set before serving.

Lime Muscovado Sugar Cookies

The tart lime frosting lends a real tang to these sugary, sophisticated cookies.

Makes 22

½ cup/1 stick/125 g butter
½ cup/100 g packed light brown sugar
1 egg, beaten
Grated peel of 1 lime
1 tbsp lime juice
Generous 2 cups/300 g all-purpose flour
1 tsp baking soda

Frosting:
Generous 1¼ cups/160 g confectioners'
   sugar
1 to 2 tbsp fresh lime juice
Grated peel of 1 lime

1. Preheat the oven to 350°F/180°C. Lightly grease two baking sheets. Cream the butter and brown sugar together until fluffy. Beat in the egg, lime peel, and juice.

2. Sift together the flour and baking soda, then beat into the butter mixture. Work together with your hands to form a soft dough.

3. On a lightly floured counter, roll out the dough to ¼ in/5 mm thick and cut out cookies with cookie cutters. Place on the baking sheets and bake until crisp and golden, 10 to 12 minutes. Let cool on the baking sheets 2 to 3 minutes, then transfer to a wire rack to cool completely.

4. To make the frosting, sift the confectioners' sugar into a bowl and stir in the lime juice and peel; mix until smooth. Spread or pipe over the cookies. Let dry for 1 to 2 hours or until the frosting has set. Store in an airtight container for up to five days.

Icebox Sugar Cookies

The chill-and-bake nature of these cookies means that you can make the dough well ahead of time and bake the cookies fresh, as you need them.

Makes 45

1¼ cups/2½ sticks/275 g butter, softened
Scant 1 cup/200 g sugar
1 egg
1 tsp vanilla extract
2⅓ cups/350 g all-purpose flour
Colored sugar sprinkles, to decorate

1. Cream the butter and sugar together until pale and fluffy. Beat in the egg and vanilla. Add the flour mix to form a soft dough.

2. Shape into a log about 2 in/5 cm thick. Spread the sugar sprinkles on a sheet of nonstick baking parchment and roll the log in the sugar until well coated.

3. Wrap the log in another sheet of baking parchment and chill until firm. At this point the dough can be stored in the refrigerator for up to one week, or placed in a plastic bag and frozen for up to two months.

4. When ready to bake, preheat the oven to 375°F/190°C. Lightly grease two baking sheets. Cut the log into slices ⅛ in/3 mm thick and arrange carefully on the baking sheets, leaving enough room for the cookies to spread.

5. Bake until just firm, 8 to 10 minutes. Let cool on the baking sheets for a few minutes before transferring to a wire rack to cool completely.

Snickerdoodles

A soft traditional cookie, with a funny name, originating from nineteenth-century New England. You could also try making wholewheat snickerdoodles by substituting 1 cup wholewheat flour for 1 cup of the all-purpose flour.

Makes 36

¾ cup/1½ sticks/175 g butter, softened
1 cup/225 g sugar
1 egg
1 tsp vanilla extract
Scant 2 cups/300 g all-purpose flour
1 tsp cream of tartar
½ tsp baking soda

To complete:
1 tbsp sugar
1 tsp ground cinnamon

1. Preheat the oven to 400°F/200°C. Ligh grease two baking sheets.

2. Cream the butter and the sugar togeth until light and fluffy. Beat in the egg and vanilla. Sift the flour, cream of tartar, and baking soda together and blend into the butter mixture to form a soft dough.

3. Break off pieces of the dough about th size of a small walnut and roll into balls. Mix the 1 tablespoon sugar and cinnamo together and roll each ball in the cinnam sugar. Arrange on the baking sheets, allowing room for the cookies to spread.

4. Bake until pale golden, about 8 to 10 minutes. Transfer to a wire rack to coc

Blueberry Thumbprint Cookies

The simple, mellow vanilla flavor of these cookies works incredibly well with the tartness of the blueberry jam. For a really traditional American taste, try filling the thumbprint well with peanut butter and jam.

Makes 36

1 cup/2 sticks/225 g butter, softened
Scant 1 cup/100 g confectioners' sugar,
  plus extra for dusting
1 tsp vanilla extract
Scant 1 cup/100 g ground almonds
Scant 1⅓ cups/200 g all-purpose flour
Blueberry jam
Confectioners' sugar, for dusting

1. Lightly grease two baking sheets. Cream the butter and sugar together until pale and fluffy, then beat in the vanilla. Blend in the ground almonds and then gradually add the flour, bringing the mixture together with your hands to form a soft dough as you add the last of the flour.

2. Lightly dust your hands with flour and roll the dough into small balls about the size of a walnut. Arrange on the baking sheets and using your thumb, make a deep hole in the center of each cookie. Chill for 30 minutes.

3. Preheat the oven to 350°F/180°C. Bake the cookies for 10 minutes, then fill each hole with a little jam and return to the oven until pale golden, about 5 minutes. Let cool on the baking sheets for a few minutes before transferring to a wire rack to cool completely. Dust with confectioners' sugar.

Spicy Cranberry Cookies

Dried cranberries can be bought sweetened or unsweetened. The dried sweetened variety resemble reddish raisins, whereas unsweetened cranberries taste slightly more tart. Choose a type to suit your particular preference.

Makes 15

½ cup/1 stick/125 g butter, softened
Scant ½ cup/100 g sugar
1 egg, separated
⅓ cup/50 g dried cranberries
1¼ cups/175 g all-purpose flour
½ tsp pumpkin pie spice
Demerara sugar, to sprinkle

1. Preheat the oven to 350°F/180°C. Lightly grease two baking sheets. Cream the butter and sugar together until light and fluffy, then beat in the egg yolk. Stir in the cranberries.

2. Sift together the flour and spice. Add to the bowl and mix to form a stiff dough. Roll out the dough on a lightly floured counter to about ⅛ in/3 mm thick and cut into 3 in/7.5 cm circles.

3. Arrange on the baking sheets. Lightly beat the egg white and brush over the surface of each circle. Sprinkle with the demerara sugar.

4. Bake until golden and brown, 15 to 18 minutes. Let cool for a few minutes on the baking sheets, then transfer to a wire rack to cool completely. Store in an airtight container for up to one week.

Brazil Nut Biscotti

Try using chopped almonds or walnuts instead of brazil nuts. Italians traditionally dunk their biscotti—a cookie native to their country—into espresso or **vin santo** *(sweet wine).*

Makes 50

2 eggs
Generous ¾ cup/175 g sugar
Grated peel 1 orange
2 tbsp orange juice
¼ cup/60 ml light vegetable oil
1⅓ cups/200 g Brazil nuts
2⅓ cups/350 g all-purpose flour
2 tsp baking powder
Scant 1 cup/175 g ground rice

1. Preheat the oven to 350°F/180°C.

2. Place the eggs and sugar in a large mixing bowl and beat until very pale and thick. Beat in the orange peel, juice, and oil. Stir in the nuts.

3. Sift the flour and baking powder together and add to the bowl with the rice, working the mixture with your hands to form a soft dough. Add a little extra flour if the dough is too sticky. Divide in half and roll out each piece to form an 8 in/20 cm log.

4. Place the logs on the baking sheets and bake until risen and golden, about 30 minutes. Remove from the oven and let cool slightly. Reduce the oven temperature to 300°F/150°C.

5. Using a serrated knife, cut the logs into thin slices and arrange on the baking sheets. Bake the slices, turning once, until crisp and golden on both sides, about 20 minutes. Store in an airtight container. These will keep for several weeks.

CHAPTER SIX

Savory Cookies

Spiced Pretzels

With a lovely spicy flavor and unusual shape, these pretzels are sure to impress guests when offered as a savory snack at a drinks party or impromptu get-together.

Makes 30

Scant 1⅓ cups/200 g all-purpose flour
½ tsp baking powder
Pinch of salt
6 tbsp butter
1 tbsp curry paste
¼ cup/50 ml boiling water
Beaten egg, to glaze

1. Preheat the oven to 350°F/180°C. Lightly grease two baking sheets.

2. Sift the flour, baking powder, and salt into a mixing bowl and rub in the butter until the mixture resembles fine breadcrumbs. Stir the curry paste into ¼ cup/50 ml boiling water, then add to the flour mixture and mix to form a soft dough.

3. Knead on a lightly floured counter until smooth. Divide into 30 pieces and roll each piece into a strand about 8 in/20 cm long. Twist into a pretzel shape by making a circle, then twisting the ends around each other to form a curved letter "B." Press into position to secure and place on the baking sheets.

4. Brush the pretzels with beaten egg. Bake until golden, 18 to 20 minutes. Carefully transfer to a wire rack to cool.

5. Store in an airtight container for one to two weeks.

Savory Whirls

You can leave these plain or top with a selection of olives, anchovies, marinated bell peppers, nuts, or sun-dried tomatoes.

Makes 15

½ cup/1 stick/125 g butter, softened
1 clove garlic, crushed
2 tbsp sour cream
Generous 1 cup/150 g all-purpose flour
½ tsp paprika
Salt and freshly ground black pepper

1. Preheat the oven to 375°F/190°C. Lightly grease two baking sheets.

2. Cream the butter until soft, then beat in the garlic, sour cream, flour, paprika, and seasoning. Mix to form a smooth paste.

3. Spoon into a pastry bag fitted with a large star tip and pipe rosettes onto the baking sheets.

4. Bake until golden, 12 to 15 minutes. Let cool on the baking sheets for a few minutes before transferring to a wire rack to cool completely.

Sesame Cheese Twists

These classic twists are a favorite at parties and look very professional—however, they are actually unbelieveably easy to make!

Makes 14

4 oz/100 g cheddar cheese
½ cup/1 stick/125 g butter, softened
Scant 1⅓ cups/200 g all-purpose flour
Beaten egg, to glaze
2 tbsp sesame seeds

1. Preheat the oven to 400°F/200°C. Lightly grease two baking sheets. Finely grate the cheese, using the fine grater attachment of a food processor.

2. Remove the grating disc and insert the metal mixing blade. Place the butter in the food processor with the cheese and process until pale and creamy. Add the flour and process until the mixture comes together to form a ball of dough.

3. Roll out the dough on a lightly floured counter to about ⅛ in/3 mm thick. Cut into strips about 6 in/15 cm long and ¼ in/5 mm wide. Take two strips at a time and twist together, pinching the ends.

4. Arrange on the baking sheets. Brush with beaten egg and sprinkle with sesame seeds. Bake until pale golden, 10 to 12 minutes. Let cool for a few minutes on the baking sheet, then transfer to a wire rack to cool completely. Store in an airtight container for up to one week.

Savory Palmier Cookies

*These cookies are so versatile—
spread them with whatever filling you
choose. A little cheese sprinkled over
the olives works well. Palmiers are
best served slightly warm, however, if
this is not possible, room temperature
is fine, too.*

Makes 20

9 oz/250 g ready-made puff pastry,
   thawed if frozen
2 tbsp pesto
Generous ¼ cup/50 g pitted black olives,
   finely chopped

1. Preheat the oven to 400°F/200°C. Roll
out the pastry on a lightly floured counter
to form a 10 x 12-in/25 x 30-cm rectangle.
Trim the edges with sharp knife.

2. Spread the pesto in a thin layer all over
the pastry, taking care to go right to the
edges. Sprinkle with the chopped olives.
With the long side facing you, fold about
3 in/7.5 cm of the shorter sides of the
pastry so that they reach about halfway
toward the center. Fold again so that they
just meet in the center. Lightly dampen the
pastry with a little water and fold again in
half down the center.

3. Using a sharp knife, cut the roll into
about 20 thin slices and arrange cut-side
down, well spaced, on the baking sheets.

4. Bake for 10 minutes, then turn them
over and bake until golden and crisp, 5 to
8 minutes. Transfer to a wire rack to cool.

Cheese and Tomato Bites

Serve these cheese-filled tomato cookies with pre-dinner drinks. Or why not pack a few into your lunchbox as a savory snack at any time of day?

Makes 30

1¼ cups/175 g all-purpose flour
½ tsp baking powder
6 tbsp butter
1 tsp celery salt, optional
2 tbsp ketchup

Filling:
Scant ½ cup/100 g cream cheese
1 tbsp snipped chives
Salt and freshly ground black pepper

1. Preheat the oven to 400°F/200°C. Lightly grease two baking sheets.

2. Place the flour and baking powder in a bowl. Rub in the butter until the mixture resembles fine breadcrumbs. Stir in the celery seeds, then add the ketchup and mix to form a stiff dough.

3. Roll out on a lightly floured counter and cut into 1 in/2.5 cm wafers with a knife or cookie cutter. Arrange on the baking sheets. Bake until golden, 10 to 12 minutes. Let cool on the baking sheets for a few minutes before transferring to a wire rack to cool completely.

4. Beat together the cream cheese and chives and season to taste. Use to sandwich two wafers together. The wafers will keep unfilled for up to one week in an airtight container; fill just prior to serving.

Oat Cakes

The oaty flavor and texture of these savory treats works very well with cheese and chutney.

Makes 12

1 cup/100 g fine oatmeal
Generous ⅓ cup/50 g all-purpose flour
1 tsp baking soda
1 tsp sugar
Pinch of salt
4 tbsp butter
1 to 2 tbsp water

1. Preheat the oven to 350°F/180°C. Lightly grease a baking sheet.

2. Put the oatmeal, flour, baking soda, sugar, and salt in a mixing bowl. Place the butter and 1 to 2 tablespoons water in a small pan and heat until the butter melts. Stir into the oatmeal mixture and combine to form a dough.

3. Turn out onto a lightly floured counter and knead until the dough is no longer sticky, adding a little extra flour if necessary.

4. Roll out the dough until ⅛ in/3 mm thick and cut out 3 in/7.5 cm circles with a cookie cutter. Arrange on the baking sheet and bake until golden, 15 to 20 minutes. Remove to a wire rack to cool. Store in an airtight container for up to two weeks.

Glossary

The following culinary terms will provide useful guidelines for international readers.

U.S.	British
All-purpose flour	Plain flour
Baking soda	Bicarbonate of soda
Beat	Whisk
Cornstarch	Cornflour
Confectioners' sugar	Icing sugar
Extract	Essence
Golden raisins	Sultanas
Graham crackers	Digestive biscuits
Jelly roll	Swiss roll
Light corn syrup	Golden syrup
Light cream	Single cream
Molasses	Black treacle
Packed brown sugar	Muscovado sugar
Pan	Tin
Peel	Zest
Plastic wrap	Cling film
Semisweet chocolate	Plain chocolate
Shredded coconut	Desiccated coconut
Sugar	Caster sugar
Wholewheat flour	Wholemeal flour

Index

Picture Credits

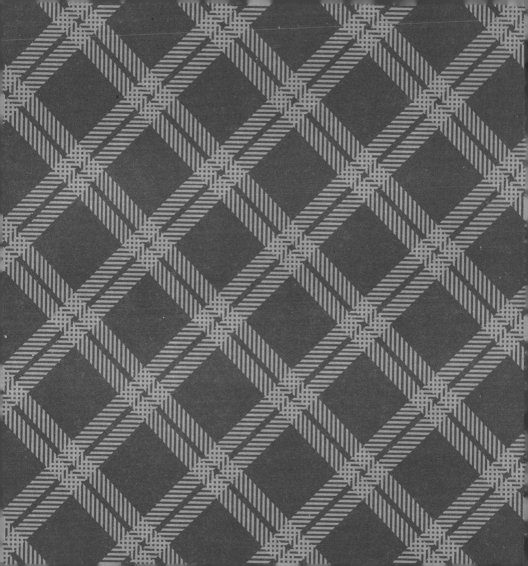